Old LOWER DEESIDE

by
David Jamieson and W. Stewart Wilson

The caption on this postcard reads 'Keith and Cairnie lady ploughing champions at Cults'. The picture was probably taken at a ploughing match at West Cults Farm in the days when Cults was still an agricultural community and not part of Aberdeen suburbia.

By the same authors:
Old Banchory
Old Royal Deeside

ACKNOWLEDGEMENTS

We would like to thank all those who have given of their local knowledge including Colin Mearns, Albert Moir, Allan Pennie and Violet Smith. Thanks are also due to Malcolm Appleby, Hugh Brodie, Alan Brotchie, Gareth Burgess, Robert Grieves, David Irvine, Nicholas Kelly, Margeorie Mekie, Victor Sang and Brian Watt who provided some of the pictures.

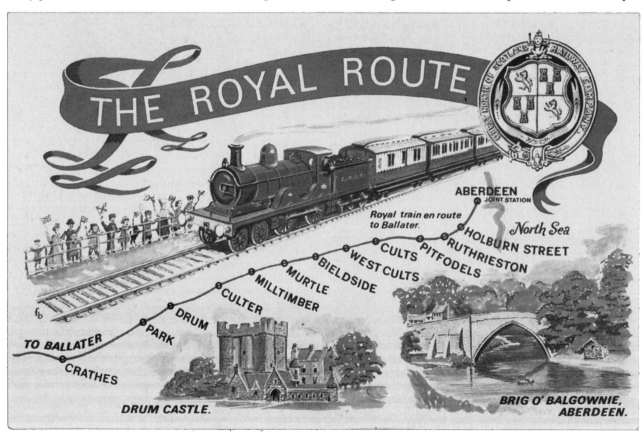

INTRODUCTION

The last ice caps finally disappeared from Deeside about 10,000 years ago and the earliest inhabitants settled there soon after that. Traces of these early settlers were found in 1905 when pygmy flints were discovered in a field at Birkwood, near Banchory. These flint implements may well date from as far back as 8500 BC. By 5500 BC the land was being farmed, and excavations which took place during the late 1970s at Balbridie, three miles east of Banchory, found traces of a remarkable timber-framed building of quite an extraordinary size. An interesting relic of probably 4000 BC is the burial cairn which can be seen on the north side of Cairn Road in Bieldside. The Romans arrived in Deeside about AD 210, when Emperor Septimius Severus forded the Dee at Tilbouries, west of Culter, and built the great marching camp of Normandykes on high ground on its north bank.

It was the coming of the new turnpike road in 1798 (replacing the old Deeside road on the north side of the Dee) and the opening in 1853 of the Deeside Railway as far as Banchory that brought a large influx of people to the area. On 7 September 1853, 200 invitations were issued for the official opening of the railway at Ferryhill station, Aberdeen. Public operation began the following day with stations at Cults, Murtle, Culter, Park, Mills of Drum and Banchory. Stations at Milltimber and Drum were provided the following year, and soon afterwards one was opened at Ruthrieston. In 1863 the private platform at Crathes Castle and the small station at Mills of Drum were closed and replaced by a new station at Crathes on the site of the old private platform. Ease of transport to Aberdeen by rail was also desired by those living south of the river, and bridges were subsequently built to provide access to stations where previously ferries and fords had been the only means of crossing the Dee.

The popularity of Deeside was enormously enhanced by Queen Victoria, who first visited the original Balmoral Castle in 1848. In 1852 the estate was bought and a new castle – completed in 1855 – was built. The Deeside Railway proved instantly popular with the royal family and on Thursday 13 October 1853, just a month after the line had opened, Queen Victoria and Prince Albert made the journey from Banchory to Ferryhill. There the Lord Provost of Aberdeen and other dignitaries met the royal party to bid them farewell to Deeside and promise them a warm welcome again. The Joint station in Aberdeen was opened in August 1854 and Ferryhill junction was then closed to passenger traffic. In subsequent years the line, extended to Aboyne in December 1859 and to Ballater in October 1866, was used

frequently by the royal family. The Shah of Persia travelled from Ferryhill to Ballater in July 1889 and in September 1896 the Czar and Czarina of Russia made the same journey.

In September 1906 King Edward VII and Queen Alexandra arrived in Aberdeen by royal train at Holburn Street station for the opening of the new buildings of Marischal College. The station was lavishly decorated for the occasion. King George V and Queen Mary alighted at Holburn Street in September 1929 on their way to the opening of the extension to the Art Gallery and Cowdray Hall. In August 1939 King George VI and family travelled up to Balmoral for the first time since his accession. On this occasion the royal train stopped at Drum for an hour so that breakfast could be served. Princesses Elizabeth and Margaret delighted the crowd that had gathered by coming out onto the platform accompanied by Queen Elizabeth. The royal family continued to use the line until its closure, with the last royal train leaving Ballater on 15 October 1965.

Following the arrival of the railway, Lower Deeside became popular with Aberdeen's merchants and businessmen who built some beautiful houses in the new commuter villages on the north bank of the Dee. With this growth in population there was an increasing need for reliable transport to the city, and the completion of the doubling of the railway track between Aberdeen and Culter in 1892 enabled a regular suburban train service to be introduced two years later. Initially there were eleven trains in each direction per day, and new stations were opened at Holburn Street, Pitfodels, and West Cults in 1894, and Bieldside in 1897. Despite services stopping at seven intermediate stations along the route, the journey from Culter to the city took a mere 21 minutes. When the suburban train service ceased in 1937 the stations opened in 1894, along with those at Ruthrieston, Bieldside, Murtle and Milltimber were closed. The closure of the rest of the line on 28 February 1966 brought to an end an important chapter of the history of Royal Deeside.

With the discovery of North Sea oil in the early 1970s Deeside saw a rapid growth in housebuilding, and became one of the most desirable places to set up home in the north-east. It is unfortunate that the decision to close the railway was taken in the 1960s – today it could have provided a most useful and convenient link to the city. However, the trackbed has been preserved and developed as a popular walkway and cycle route from Duthie Park in Aberdeen to Culter.

Entitled 'Aberdeen from Balnagask', this view was taken from the south shore of the Dee and looks north over the harbour towards the towers and spires of Aberdeen. The city's docks were developed in the early nineteenth century, before which the mouth of the Dee was wide and shallow with exposed sandbanks at low tide. The north pier was constructed in 1781 by David Smeaton, but extensive further dredging work was required in the early nineteenth century (supervised by Thomas Telford) to create the Victoria Dock and Albert Basin. As a result of these works the Dee was diverted to the more southerly channel along which it flows today. From the Middle Ages Aberdeen was a centre for the export of goods from the north-east of Scotland with woollen items, linen and granite shipped mainly to Europe. The creation of the docks encouraged growth in shipbuilding in the nineteenth century, and in the 1860s the wood and iron clipper *Thermopylae* was constructed for the tea trade to China; she famously defeated the Clyde-built *Cutty Sark* for speed. The herring fleet numbered over 450 boats in the late 1880s but gradually gave way to the white fish industry. At its height a century ago there were some 200 trawlers providing work for over 25,000 people on- and offshore. Now the harbour area is crowded with supply boats and other craft servicing the North Sea oil industry.

The Dee is famed as one of Scotland's great salmon rivers, and anglers continue to use their skills on the many beats on the river today. During the nineteenth century, however, there was controversy over the effect of the netting at the river's mouth. As early as 1833 the *New Statistical Account* for Maryculter reported that 'the part of the Dee opposite to the parish formerly let at high rents for salmon-fishing . . . now will not repay the fisherman's wages, owing to the stake and bay-nets at the mouth of the river'. By then salmon packed in ice could be transported by ship to the London market and provided a lucrative return for net fishers, some of whom are seen here.

The Aberdeen burgh records of 1648 refer to a ferry at the entrance to the harbour for the use of those wanting to cross the river to and from Torry. On 5 April 1876, while the river was in spate, a ferry overloaded with holidaymakers returning from a day trip to the Bay of Nigg sank with the loss of 32 lives. The *Aberdeen Journal* reported that 'On the fateful journey there were some 80 people on board, well in excess of the number allowed to be carried. When [the ferry] left the gunwale was seen to be only a few inches from the water's edge'. The youngest victim was a boy of nine years. This tragedy led to demands for a safer means of crossing the river and hence the building of the Victoria Bridge five years later.

The Wellington Suspension Bridge, known locally as the Chain Bridge, was designed by Samuel Brown and named after the Duke of Wellington. It was opened in 1830 at a cost of £10,831 and replaced the old ferry of Craiglug. The bridge provided the only link to Torry until 1881 when more direct access was gained by means of the Victoria Bridge. Designed by Edward Blyth, the latter also carried gas and water across the river, helping to establish Torry as a new southern suburb of Aberdeen. The Chain Bridge ceased to carry vehicular traffic following the opening of the Queen Elizabeth II Bridge in 1984, but continued to be used as a footbridge for a time.

YACHTING POND, DUTHIE PARK, ABERDEEN

Situated on the north side of the Dee and covering 44 acres, Duthie Park was presented to the city by Miss Elizabeth Crombie Duthie of Ruthrieston and laid out at a cost of £50,000. The park was opened by Princess Beatrice, the youngest daughter of Queen Victoria, on 27 September 1883 when a public holiday was declared. After touring the park Princess Beatrice left for Balmoral by train using a specially constructed platform near the Mound (the name given to the hillock made up of earth excavated during the digging out of the ponds). The original Palm House or Winter Gardens was erected in 1899 and continues to offer residents of Aberdeen a place of relaxation. More recently the Mound has been planted with over 100,000 rose bushes, thus establishing Aberdeen as an important rose centre.

The old Bridge of Dee was the principal point of access to the city from the south. It was conceived by Bishop Elphinstone in the late fifteenth century, but it was one of his successors, Bishop Gavin Dunbar, who saw the plans to fruition. Building work started in 1520 and the bridge was completed in 1527. It carries a number of appropriate coats of arms and commemorative inscriptions which are incorporated into the piers. Soon after completion a chapel for travellers was added at the north end, and in 1545 a large gateway was built at the southern end which served as a toll gate. The bridge has been altered many times over the years, and in 1842 was widened to 26 feet from its original 14½ feet. In 1941 an additional bridge over the Dee, the King George VI Bridge, was built a short distance downstream, and this has relieved some of the pressure caused by the much increased volumes of traffic entering the city from the south in recent years. In the foreground is the start of the South Deeside Road, described by G. M. Fraser in *The Old Deeside Road* as 'less important than the North Deeside Road for its admirable quality and convenience for the public' but nonetheless 'superior to it, on the whole, for its charming scenery and outlook'.

The present Banchory House, the most easterly of several large estate houses on the South Deeside Road, was built in 1840 in the parish of Banchory Devenick. It was designed by the Aberdeen architect John 'Tudor Johnny' Smith in imitation of an extension added in 1830 to the original Balmoral Castle. His son, William Smith, was the architect of the rebuilt Balmoral Castle in 1854. Within the grounds of Banchory House there is a monument in commemoration of HRH Prince Albert's visit in 1859.

The lands of Banchory House were originally granted in 1244 by Alexander II to the Abbot and Convent of Arbroath and passed through various families until they were bought in 1872 by John Stewart, an Aberdeen comb manufacturer. The interior of the house was devastated by fire in 1978, but following restoration Banchory House now forms part of the Camphill Community and is known as Beannachar. Sent on 14 February 1914 by 'Mary – with love', perhaps as a Valentine greeting, this postcard features the female servants of Banchory House at the time.

St Devenick's Bridge, more commonly known as 'Shakkin' Briggie', was built in 1837 at a cost of £1,400 using funds provided by Dr George Morison, minister of Banchory Devenick Church from 1785 to 1845. His parish extended over both sides of the Dee and the bridge replaced a boat which carried parishioners from the north side of the river to the church on the south. When the Dee was in spate, excuses for non-attendance were frequent and the minister had the bridge built to ensure a full congregation. It was said of the design by John Smith, its architect, that 'the bridge had such a degree of firmness that its motion was scarcely perceptible in the heaviest gales of wind', although its unofficial name suggested that the description wasn't true! The floods of 1958 ruined the bridge's foundations, after which it was closed. No funds have since been made available to restore it.

Cults Bowling Club was formed in April 1887 and for the first ten years of its existence played on land belonging to Edmund Geering of Dunmail. In April 1896 the club was offered ground at Meadowbank (shown in this picture) and plans were drawn up for a bowling green and tennis court. There is no evidence, however, of tennis ever being played there. At first the club made do with the original clubhouse which was brought from Dunmail, but in 1913 a new pavilion was built at a cost of £118! This underwent many extensions and improvements over the next 70 years. In the 1990s the club embarked on major renovations, and today can boast a first-class green with floodlighting allowing play to take place after dark.

This view of the hotel and post office in Cults dates from the early years of the twentieth century, and was taken shortly after the introduction of the tram service from Mannofield through Cults to Bieldside in 1904. On account of the sharpness of the bend, the trams had to reduce their speed at the corner beside the Cults Burn from the normal 12 mph to a more modest speed. Once an old coaching inn of two storeys, the Cults Hotel incorporated a grocer's shop licensed to sell wines, porter and ales. The wooden stairway to the hotel's left is outside what was once the premises of the local blacksmith, while beyond that the roof of the Cults pumping station can be seen. The old turnpike road of 1798 survives today as the lay-by in front of the hotel. To its right in this picture are the post office and general store which date from 1901.

Born c.1866, William Wade Gorrod was indentured to Messrs Kemp & Walker, millers and grain merchants in Aberdeen and in 1888, when he was in his twenties, became a partner with George Davie in the firm of Messrs Gorrod & Davie, millers and grain merchants, based at the old mill at Cults. Some time later the firm amalgamated with Kemp & Walker & Co. of King Street in Aberdeen to become Gorrod, Davie, Kemp, Walker & Co. Ltd. The old mill at Cults is situated in Millden Road, opposite the Cults Hotel (seen in the upper picture). It continued to be used as a mill until the 1960s, and having been sold in 1978 was converted into a private house.

ockey Match in the Allan Park, Cults

In 1897 David Allan, an Aberdeen cabinetmaker and resident of West Cults, gifted six acres of land to the Parish of Peterculter (of which Cults was part at that time). On 26 June that year Allan Park was officially opened to commemorate the diamond jubilee of Queen Victoria. It was laid out for football and hockey in the winter and for cricket and tennis in the summer. The adjoining pond was used for skating and curling when weather conditions permitted. Here a ladies hockey match is in progress *c*.1900, with the players wearing full-length skirts. Unfortunately, the pond has become very overgrown in recent years.

In the early years of the last century it was quite common to use postcards to send Christmas greetings, and this view of the Square in Cults bears the message 'Wishing you all a Happy Christmas'. At one time the only shop in Cults was situated at the hotel, but during the final twenty years of the nineteenth century the village gradually expanded to the west along the North Deeside Road, and more business premises were opened in that vicinity. The names of many of these businesses have long disappeared, but among others older locals will remember Wishart the butcher, whose shop is in the right foreground of this view. Further from the camera, with a mortar and pestle above the door, is John R. Reith's chemists.

One of the oldest businesses in the area is undoubtedly Kelly of Cults. Benjamin Kelly established his bakery in 1902 and used horse-drawn carts to serve outlying areas. There was a tea-room behind the shop down St Devenick's Place where customers could enjoy the firm's wide range of fancy cakes. In 1930 Benjamin's son Bruce took over the running of the company, building up a fleet of a dozen vans delivering bakery goods and groceries. He even serviced the vehicles himself in a garage located where the shop car park is now situated. Major expansion took place in 1955 and in 1966 the firm established the largest self-service grocery store in the Aberdeen area. A serious fire in 1977 saw the rebuilding of the present supermarket which is still under the management of the Kelly family.

The Aberdeen Suburban Tramways Company was formed at the beginning of the twentieth century, and the route officially opened on Thursday 23 June 1904 when the first tram ran from Mannofield in Aberdeen to Bieldside. (The Board of Trade inspection had taken place two days beforehand, with trial runs commencing on 18 June.) This picture shows car No. 5 at Bieldside terminus, displaying an advertisement for Isdale & McCallum's soap powder. It had been hoped that the tramway would be extended to Culter, but the plans were never realised. Some trams only ran as far as Mannofield, where there was a depot (now the site of a petrol filling station), while others continued to Castle Street in Aberdeen. Timing on the Suburban Company's tram route was all-important as the line was single track, with passing places at intervals. The last tram had run by 2 July 1927, by which time the track and rolling stock had deteriorated so badly that it was not uncommon for a tram to be derailed several times on one journey. The tower of St Devenick's Episcopal Church, built in 1903, is in the background of the picture.

In the early twentieth century the surface of the road through Bieldside was still very rough, and the bicycle was a popular means of transport.

Long before the withdrawal of the trams in 1927, the Aberdeen Suburban Tramways Company had begun to invest in buses. It purchased three petrol-electric vehicles in 1914 to provide a regular service from Bieldside to Culter, but with the outbreak of war that year these were instead used to transfer wounded soldiers between Aberdeen hospitals. After the war, together with many other operators, the company offered tours to beauty spots on Deeside. In 1925 the first moves were made to provide a bus service on the route operated by the trams between Aberdeen and Bieldside. Many 'pirate' operators introduced rival services, including Bydand Motor Transport which ran buses from Union Terrace in Aberdeen to Bieldside. The Aberdeen Suburban Transport Company Ltd. (formed from the former tramway company) answered back and fierce competition existed until October 1932 when W. Alexander of Falkirk acquired both Bydand and the Suburban Co. Among the pirate vehicles used on the route between Aberdeen and Culter was RS 8305, a 30/60 hp Albion bus new in 1926 with bodywork by Cowieson of Glasgow. It was operated by Major Sibley's Gordon Line, and the notices on the windows indicate fares to various destinations from Aberdeen: threepence to Bieldside; fourpence to Milltimber; and fivepence to Culter Square.

Bieldside station was built to meet the needs of commuters who were moving to the new residential districts being developed around Aberdeen at the end of the nineteenth century. It was opened on 1 June 1897 and commanded one of the best views in the district. The stationmaster's house is on the right in this picture. Deeside Golf Club lies to the south, and in the early days, before car ownership became more common, many golfers used the train service from Aberdeen to get to and from the golf course, which was laid out immediately adjacent to the station.

The inaugural meeting to consider the formation of a golf club at Bieldside was held on 24 November 1902 in Cults School, when a 'rather small attendance' was reported. Haughton Farm, close to Bieldside station, was considered to be suitable for conversion to a nine-hole course, and was leased for twenty years at a rent of £80. By the time Deeside Golf Club was opened on 5 September 1903 membership had reached 240 people, with fees set at one guinea per annum for gentlemen and fifteen shillings for ladies and juniors. The clubhouse was built a year later at a cost of £700, and soon afterwards the course was extended to eighteen holes. It has seen many changes since then, but still commands some fine views to the south which include, amongst other landmarks, the former Blairs College and Ardoe House.

The estate of Ardoe, on the south side of the Dee, was bought in 1839 by Alexander Ogston, and the house of the same name was designed and built in 1878 for his son Alexander 'Soapie' Ogston, an Aberdeen soap magnate. As a baronial mansion it was reputed to rival Balmoral Castle, and remained in the family until 1945. It was then converted to a hotel with fifteen rooms, but has been expanded considerably over the past 50 years to a complex of over 100 rooms.

ARDOE HOUSE HOTEL NEAR ABERDEEN.

Blairs College and Chapel, Deeside.

In 1827 the Blairs estate was gifted by the Menzies family of Pitfodels to the bishops of the Roman Catholic Church so that the mansion house could be used as a seminary for candidates for the priesthood. Students were transferred from the existing seminary at Aquhorthies, near Inverurie, on 2 June 1829, the year of full Catholic emancipation. It was reported that 'on that day the whole family, superiors and students (twenty-six in number) came down to Inverury [sic] and took the fly-boat on the canal to Aberdeen. After dining at George Hay's Queen Street, they arrived about 5 p.m. in five carriages at Blairs.' During the nineteenth century the average number of students attending the seminary was around 50, with three priests as tutors. 1,836 boys were enrolled at Blair College during the first 100 years of its existence, and over a third went on to become priests. A boarding school, the Roman Catholic College of St Mary's, was opened in 1897 and had accommodation for 200 students. A chapel was added in 1901, and although the college closed in 1986 due to a lack of pupils the chapel continues to function. Planning applications for major developments of the college site have not so far been successful.

Looking towards Blairs College from Bieldside on the north bank of the Dee. A ferry operated across the river at this point, charging a fare of one penny, and some of the priests used it to take them to the Deeside Golf Club's course. There they would start at the old 6th hole and after a break for refreshment at the club-house complete their round at the 5th green before catching the ferry back to Blairs.

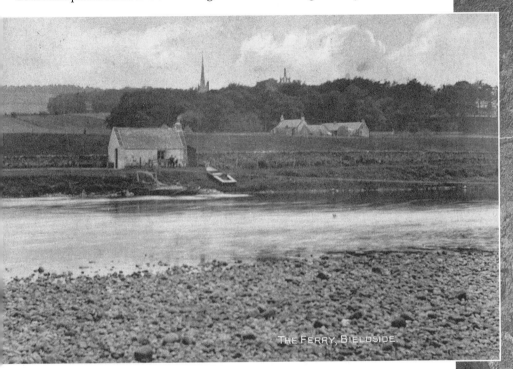

THE FERRY, BIELDSIDE.

HEATHCOT FERRY MAN.

The crossing, sometimes known as the Heathcot Ferry, was operated by the Main family from the early days of the twentieth century. The *Third Statistical Account* for Maryculter mentions that Inch of Auchlunies was later renamed Inch of Heathcot. In 1774 this was an island, but had become joined to the north bank of the river by 1850 and is now part of Deeside Golf Club (though remaining in Maryculter Parish). On the death of her father, Bella Main – or 'Ferry Bell' as she was affectionately known – took over the running of the ferry. After it ceased operating in the early 1960s she continued to run her tea-room in the little cottage on the south bank of the river for at least another ten years.

In 1894 the Great North of Scotland Railway Company instituted its suburban service along what by that time was the double track between Aberdeen and Culter. That year new stations were opened at Holburn Street, Pitfodels and West Cults. Murtle (pictured here) was one of the original stations on the line to Banchory and opened in September 1853. When the suburban service was withdrawn on 5 April 1937 it was closed along with another six of the intermediate stations. This then left Cults as the only stop between Culter and Aberdeen. The old station is now a private house. There is mention of Murtle as early as 1163 when the Barony of Murtle was granted by Malcolm IV to the Bishop of Aberdeen. Murtle gets its name from the Gaelic *mor-tulach* – the great knoll – and it is on that knoll that Murtle House was built for John Thurburn to the design of the architect Archibald Simpson. One of the finest classical houses on Deeside, it now forms part of the Rudolf Steiner School.

The Deeside Hydropathic was built in 1899 about half a mile to the north of Murtle station. It replaced Heathcot on the south side of the Dee which had been used as a hydropathic hotel for about 30 years. Hydropathy, defined as the treatment of disorders by the external and internal application of water, originated in Austria in the 1830s and subsequently spread to Britain. Treatment generally took place in specially-built hotels such as this one, and Deeside's new hydropathic was a large and imposing building which originally had about 100 bedrooms. From its high elevation it commanded some wonderful views over lower Deeside. The pools in the nearby Murtle Den were originally stocked with trout to provide fishing for visitors. Later the building was renamed Tor-na-Dee and in 1945 the Scottish Red Cross bought it for the treatment of ex-servicemen and women suffering from pulmonary tuberculosis. When the need for such establishments dwindled the Scottish Red Cross transferred ownership of the building to the National Health Service. In May 1964, during the typhoid fever epidemic in Aberdeen, it was used as an isolation hospital. Until recently it was a convalescent hospital but it has now closed and its future is uncertain.

MILLTIMBER STATIO[N]

Milltimber station became better used after the building of the Mill Inn Bridge in 1895, which allowed residents on the south bank of the Dee to gain access to the railway. A London & North Eastern Railway advertisement of 1936 gave details of special trains which were being run from Inverurie and Aberdeen to Milltimber for the Boy Scouts' Rally at Templars Park on 26 September, when Lord Baden-Powell opened the City of Aberdeen camping ground. Here a 'Subbie' (as trains on the suburban service were fondly known) passes another train at Milltimber. The message on the reverse of the postcard, written at the station on 8 April 1915, recalls that it was on 'the 10 April that the Titanic sailed on her fateful voyage [three years earlier] – I will not say more just now'. One can only speculate as to the writer's reasons for including this curious statement on the card.

THE MILL INN BRIDGE, MARYCULTER.

A. 4056.

The two parishes of Peterculter and Maryculter, situated on the north and south sides of the river respectively, date from the late thirteenth century when the Templar Church of St Mary was accepted as a parish church for the living south of the river. The parishes were linked both by ferry and the Coblestock ford until the structure now known as Maryculter Bridge (originally Mill Inn Bridge) was built in 1895. Opened by Mrs A. M. Ogston of Ardoe, this provided easy access to Milltimber station from the south. The potential value of the bridge to the local community is illustrated by the plaque it carries listing the subscribers of funds. In addition to public subscriptions, monies were provided by Kincardineshire County Council, Aberdeenshire County Council, the Town Council of Aberdeen and the Great North of Scotland Railway. At the height of the great spate of 25 January 1937 the road on the bridge was under four feet of water.

The earliest part of Kingcausie House dates from the sixteenth century, and was built on lands acquired by the Irvine family of Drum from the Knights of St John in 1535. The Irvine lairds have many stories told about them including John, the second laird, who when aged 80 fell in love with and married a girl of sixteen. The house was extended by the architect David Bryce in 1853, and is one of his finest compositions. It is recorded that Queen Victoria so admired its 'Abbotsford like facade' that she asked for the royal train to be halted so that she could view it across the river. The house remains in the possession of the Irvine-Fortescue family, descendants of the original Irvine family, after fifteen generations.

THE MILL INN, MARYCULTER.

A.4055.

The Mill Inn at Maryculter was one of the most popular inns on Deeside for travellers from Aberdeen, so much so that the Mill of Maryculter Friendly Society was established there in 1830. Its members were drawn from the professional classes and businessmen of Aberdeen, and met and dined together at least once a year. Also known as the Maryculter Club, its meetings were not always held at the inn, however, and the club's last dinner took place at Alford in 1859. The former corn mill is now an antique shop and its waterwheel is presently being restored.

"ON THE BANKS O' THE SILVERY DEE"
LYNN PARK TEA ROOMS AND RECREATION GROUND
EIGHT MILES FROM ABERDEEN ON SOUTH DEESIDE.

Lynn Park tearooms and recreation ground was opened in 1925 in a field provided at an annual rent of £10 by the 13th Laird of Kingcausie, William Archer Irvine-Fortescue. It was situated opposite the old Mill Inn and proved a very popular place for picnics and days out. The recreation ground had tennis courts and swings and a local farmer used to take children in a rowing boat round the pond. In 1939, on the outbreak of war, the army requisitioned the park and built huts and stables there. These were used by men from the Indian army (whose mules were also stabled there) and later accommodated Polish and Ukrainian soldiers. The huts were demolished after the war.

Corbie Lynn, Maryculter, Deeside.

The Corbie Lynn and Crynoch Burn, noted beauty spots, have provided many local stories. The 7th Laird of Kingcausie sought to obtain a fabulous pot of gold here, and is said to have been frustrated by the local water kelpie. Sir Godfrey Wedderburn, a Knight Templar, took his own life at the Lynn on returning from the Crusades. A Saracen lady who had saved his life followed him back and when she appeared to the Templars he was condemned to death – despite his protestations that their relationship was platonic. He committed suicide and she followed suit. Now the recently developed Storybook Glen has different fables to tell.

Maryculter House, Deeside.

The Knights Templars were granted lands in the vicinity of Maryculter House by William the Lion, King of Scots, in 1187, and a later chapel was dedicated to their patron saint, St Mary. This is now in a fairly ruinous condition although the Ha' Hoose of Maryculter, dating from the seventeenth century, has been incorporated into the present Maryculter House. From 1618 the estate was in the ownership of the Menzies family, and in 1811 was bought by the Gordons of Fyvie. Sir Cosmo Duff Gordon inherited it in 1896 and in 1912 was one of only a few people to be rescued from the *Titanic*. Many stories have been told of how he came to survive, but afterwards he seems to have become something of a recluse at Maryculter. On his death in 1935 the estate was broken up and sold. After the war the old mansion house was converted into a hotel, while some 25 acres of the grounds were bought by the Boy Scouts' Association of Aberdeen. This has been developed into an excellent camping ground known as Templars' Park, and is still in the ownership of the Aberdeen Scout Association. Prior to 1936 the north bank of the river could be reached by a ferry which departed from near Maryculter House. The ferrywoman – Margaret Irvine or Boatie Maggie – would take passengers to the churchyard on the Peterculter side of the river for a fare of one penny.

Early in the thirteenth century the extensive lands of Culter – situated along both banks of the river – formed part of the possessions of the powerful Durward family (the hereditary door-wards to the kings of Scotland, hence their name). In 1247 lands on the north bank were given to Robert Wauchope by Alexander II. A chapel dedicated to St Peter had already been built there by the Durwards. By the end of that century these lands had passed to the Cumin family, one of whom married the granddaughter of Robert Wauchope. Culter House, the Ha' Hoose of the Cumins, was built *c.*1650 a little to the north-east of what is now Peterculter and replaced an earlier house on the same site. Above the entrance on the south front is the family's coat of arms comprising two ostrich supporters bearing the family crest with its three sheaves of corn and the motto 'Courage'. The Cumins appear to have been both extravagant and eccentric: one laird had his horse shod with silver shoes when he attended the marriage of Mary, Queen of Scots and in 1729 the 15th Laird was persuaded by a dream of his wife's to visit the Cherokee Indians in America. He came back their chief and lawgiver, but by this time was bankrupt and the estate had been acquired by the lawyer Patrick Duff. It was sold in 1908 to Theodore Crombie of Grandholm, but in 1910 the house was badly damaged by fire. During the renovations two wings were added. Dr A. Marshall Mackenzie, a notable Aberdeen architect, purchased the house and grounds in 1924 and in 1938 it became the home of Dr Theodore Watt. In 1946 St Margaret's School for Girls acquired the property and used it as a house for their boarders for the next 40 years, after which it reverted to private occupation.

This view of Culter from Burnside shows thatched cottages in the foreground, with the railway line and goods yard in the middle distance and a branch line leading to Culter Paper Mills. A few granite-built villas overlook the railway line, while behind them on the skyline is the tower of the Free Church, opened in 1895 and later known as Kelman Memorial Church. Opposite the church in what was then called Church Terrace – now the main Deeside road through Culter – is a terrace of tenements.

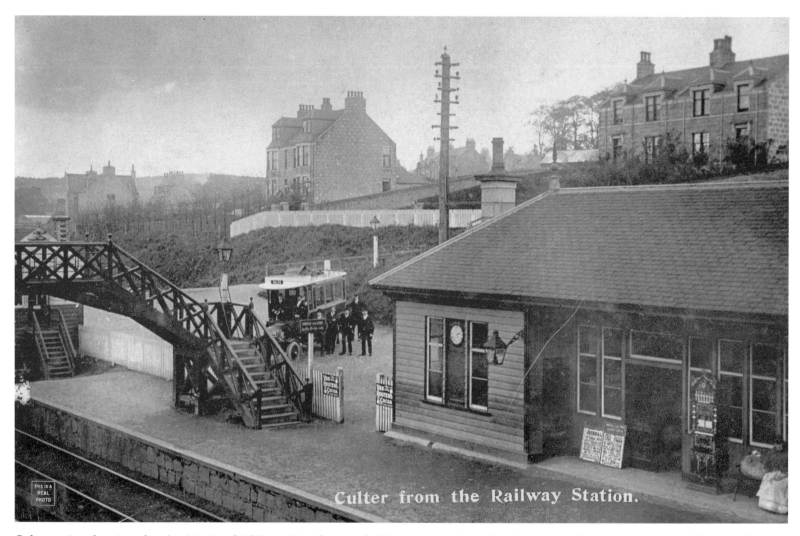

THIS IS A REAL PHOTO

Culter from the Railway Station.

Culter station showing a bus (registration SA 74) awaiting the arrival of the next train from Aberdeen, some of whose passengers will be taken by road to Midmar, twelve miles to the north-west. This service was operated by the Great North of Scotland Railway from June 1905 until November 1906 when it was replaced by a direct bus service from Aberdeen. Above the station are the two granite villas of East Brae and West Brae.

The turnpike road through Culter was constructed in 1798, but even when this postcard was produced in the early years of the twentieth century the road surface was still very rough. The tall building on the right known as Coronation Buildings was constructed to mark the coronation of King Edward VII. Further along the road on the right the gable end of the Gordon Arms Hotel (built in 1899 and demolished in 2002 to make way for flats) can just be seen, and behind that the chimney of the paper mill.

Families in their Sunday best walk through Culter along a main road deserted except for a solitary motorcycle and sidecar. The top of tower of the church can just be made out on the left, along with the public hall (with its oval window) built in 1886 for the convenience of the community and purchased by James Adams in 1924. It was acquired by the Freemasons (Lodge Leuchar 1224) in 1928 as the local Masonic hall. Part of it is now used as a shop. Situated next to the public hall on its east (far) side, where the Royal Bank of Scotland now stands, was the wooden 'bichty' (bicycle shed) belonging to the Culter Cycling Club. West of the hall and nearer the camera are the houses Shamrock Cottage and Ben Ledi, followed by Carnie's Cottage where Miss Keith had her draper's shop. The impressive granite house known as Carnie's Building (bearing the date 1903) is next in line, whilst to its left is Culter Recreation Hall, a converted wooden army hut bought in 1922. This was used as an ex-servicemen's club and in 1947 became the community centre. Over the years it has been added to and improved and still maintains its place as a focal point for many activities in Culter.

Unlike the other villages on Deeside, Culter owed its early development to industry rather than tourism and commuting. Bartholomew Smith began the manufacture of paper here in 1751, advertising for rags in the *Aberdeen Journal* and going to the city on Fridays to collect them. The pure iron-free water of the Culter Burn was ideal for paper manufacturing, and a ready market was quickly established for the mill's products. In 1819 the Smith family sold the business, which changed hands several times before being acquired by Messrs Pirie & Sons of Stoneywood in 1856. John Johnston was retained as manager after the takeover. The Culter Mills Paper Company was floated in 1865, with John Johnston appointed as managing director; he was succeeded as manager by his son J. W. Johnston. The family was held in high regard (Johnston Gardens in Culter is named after them), and it was J. W. Johnston who set up the Public Hall Limited Liability Company in 1885 enabling the public hall to be built. In 1882 James Lawrence Geddes joined Culter Mills and had a notable career as secretary, manager and finally chairman of directors. The Geddes family were associated with the mill for many years, but the difficult economic conditions of the late 1970s led to its decline, with the mill hooter sounding for the last time at noon on Friday 13 February 1981. The old mill is now the site of a major housing development.

The Culter Mills Paper Co. was known for looking after both its workers and the local community. In 1888 the company built two blocks of houses for employees, and in 1915 purchased four acres of ground at Malcolm Road where 'substantial and convenient' cottages were also built for staff. In 1920 the company acquired ground near the school where a bowling green, putting green and three tennis courts were laid out for the use of mill-workers and others in the district. The recreation ground was officially opened in 1923 by J. Fraser Geddes, the mill's general manager. The bowling green is still well used but the tennis courts have long since fallen into disuse.

On 1 September 1896 Craigton Higher Grade School (illustrated here) was opened in Culter with 172 pupils in attendance, providing a badly needed replacement for the old Craigton Public School. The roll soon increased and by 1907 a second floor had been added. During the alterations some classes were transferred to the public hall. On 22 June 1926 the school changed its name to Culter Higher Grade School, and in 1960 the first proposals were made to convert it into a two-stream primary school and erect a secondary school on a separate site. After careful study of population projections these plans fell through, and instead it was in Cults that a new secondary school was built. Cults Academy opened on 31 October 1966 when 248 secondary pupils and 25 members of staff transferred from Culter. From then on Culter provided education only for pupils of primary school age.

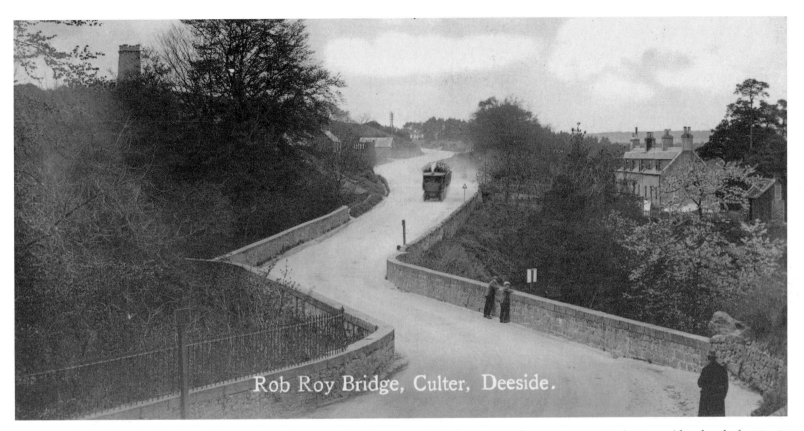

Rob Roy Bridge, Culter, Deeside.

Just above the bridge over the Culter Burn is the picturesque Den of Culter, which was dammed to create a reservoir to provide a head of water to drive the mills. Writing in the early nineteenth century, the then minister of Peterculter, Revd George Mark, described it thus: 'The reservoir contains one of the largest artificially collected bodies of water anywhere. It is confined in the den above the bridge by a large dike at its mouth, between its opposing rocky sides. When full, it is nearly 20 feet deep, and extends in length about half a mile. The aqueduct from this reservoir to the mill wheel is a work of considerable extent, and deserves notice. It is composed of wood, is 700 feet long, 7 feet wide, and deep, and is supported on stone pillars neatly built, with iron and wooden pillars between. It passes below the bridge crossing the burn, about 10 feet above its surface, and conveys a large body of water.' The cottages on the right of this picture are known as Clayhills, and Miss Jessie Thomson, who lived in one of them, unveiled the 1926 statue of Rob Roy. On the hill to the left stands the monument which was 'Erected in proud and grateful memory of the men from this district who fell in the Great War 1914–1918', to which has been added the names of those who died in the Second World War. A lady called 'Pie Jean' had a shop across the bridge near where the Italian restaurant is situated today. This was a popular meeting place for locals, where for nine old pence you could have a pie and peas and a cup of tea!

Kennerty Mills, Culter

There were once numerous oatmeal mills in the Culter area. In 1917 John Gavin took over the Upper Mill at Kennerty (dating from 1838 and shown here) from the Laird of Drum. His son William took over the business in 1923, and the mill was subsequently modernised. By 1975 it was the last surviving meal mill in the area. William Gavin bought the Murtle Mill (now a restaurant) in 1938 and in 1940 acquired the derelict mill at Lower Kennerty. At the time there was a great demand for oatmeal for the armed forces, and having been restored the mill produced 30 tons of meal a week which was sent to Aberdeen to be packed into seven pound tins. Some time later the Lower Kennerty Mill was converted into a house, initially for Mr Gavin's daughter Evelyn. A fourth mill at Wardmill on the Gormack Burn was also owned by William Gavin, who retired in 1970.

H. Coy. 7th G. H. (Culter) Leaving for War service 6/8/14

On 6 August 1914, just three days after the outbreak of the First World War, H Company 7th Gordon Highlanders (Culter) marched down Malcolm Road to the station and then travelled by train to Bedford. Circled in this picture is Alex 'Fitchie' McDonald, a papermaker at the local mill. Eleven Gordon battalions and 50,000 of all ranks fought on the western front, and over 8,900 lost their lives. The Culter war memorial records the names of 60 men from the district who fell in the First World War, among whom are ten men of H Company 7th Gordon Highlanders.

May Wallie
Culter

In pagan times wells and springs were regarded as bringers of health from the heart of the earth. It was customary to make pilgrimages to them, particularly on Beltane Day – 1 May – when people would gather in the early morning before sunrise to observe certain rituals. These included walking three times round the well and silvering the water by throwing in a silver coin before drinking from it and making a wish. Visitors would leave a fragment of clothing or a pin behind, thus casting off cares which would transfer to anyone who picked up the cloth or pin. The May Wallie at Culter, illustrated here sometime before the First World War, was such an event. People would rise at 6 a.m. and walk up Malcolm Road to the well on the banks of the Leuchar Burn between North Linn and Denmill, where they would drink the iron-tasting water and make a wish. The custom continued right up to middle of last century.

Looking north from Newmill, Culter. There has been a farm at Newmill since the seventeenth century, whilst a sawmill and meal mill, both driven by water from the Culter Burn, were once situated here. The meal mill can be seen to the right of the farmhouse, with the sawmill further to the right again. Apple Cottage, the little cottage on the left beside the haystacks, was the miller's house. When Charlie Smith, the great grandfather of the present owner, arrived as sawmiller for the Culter estate he first stayed at Cornyhaugh up the hill on the opposite side of the burn. Above that was the tip for the paper mill and also Crombie Park, the football ground of Culter FC. The farm in the distance on the left is Lower Craigton.

Drum Castle was the home of the Irvine family from the fourteenth century. The charter granting them the forest of Drum was given to William de Irwin by Robert the Bruce on 1 February 1322/3, and on 4 October 1323 the Free Barony of Drum was created. This was possibly bestowed on William de Irwin as a reward for his services in the royal chancellery under the patronage of the influential Bernard, Abbot of Arbroath. It is believed that the Tower of Drum was built by Richard Cementarius, Provost of Aberdeen in the thirteenth century, and was used as a lodge by successive kings who came to hunt in the forest that surrounded the tower. With its entrance doorway at first floor level (which in times past was reached by a movable ladder) the great tower was perhaps built to defend a strategic ford across the River Dee. An adjoining wing was added to the tower in 1619 and forms a sharp contrast to the grim keep. With its crow-stepping and corbelling, it is typical of the Scottish architecture of the time. On the death in 1975 of the 24th Laird, Henry Quentin Forbes Irvine, the property was acquired by the National Trust for Scotland.

The old church of Drumoak was situated at Dalmaik close to the river and the line of the old Deeside road. The church site and burial ground date from around 1062 and the present ruins are of a building probably constructed in the mid-seventeenth century. During the eighteenth century changes were made to the south wall to allow for the repositioning of the pulpit on that wall. At the same time a gallery was built on the east wall served by an outside stair (visible in the picture). The well-known Gregory family are associated with Drumoak. John Gregory was the minister at Dalmaik and his son James, born in the manse in November 1638, went on to become professor of mathematics first at the University of St Andrews and later at Edinburgh. He also designed the first practical reflecting telescope. Over the next 200 years the Gregory family provided no fewer than fourteen professors of mathematics, philosophy or medicine to Scottish and English universities. A great-grandson of James, also called James, became professor of medicine at Edinburgh University in 1776 and was responsible for 'Gregory's Mixture' a well-known laxative of the day. When the new turnpike road was built in 1798 a church was needed nearer the centre of the parish, and in 1836 a new place of worship was built in Drumoak itself.

When Robert the Bruce granted the park and royal forest of Drum to the Irvine family he reserved certain rights for himself. His grandson, Robert II, gave the whole of the park to the Irvines in 1389 and it remained in their possession until 1737. Thereafter it became known as the Estate of Park and had several owners. The mansion house of Park was erected in 1822 and is an excellent example of Archibald Simpson's work. It can't be seen from the North Deeside Road and is best viewed from across the river. In 1839 Alexander John Low became proprietor under rather unusual circumstances. James Kinloch, a native of Kincardineshire who had made his fortune in India, died a bachelor and left a substantial sum of money to the family of his sister, a Mrs Low, on the understanding that it would be invested in the purchase of land in Scotland and that his heir would assume the name of Kinloch. Hence Alexander Low became a Kinloch. On 5 July 1852 his wife cut the first turf for the building of the Deeside Railway on land close to Park House.

It was through the generosity of Alexander Kinloch, Laird of Park, that land was given for the building of the Free Church (opened 1880) in Park village. Although this united with the Parish Church up the hill in Drumoak in 1934, services continued to be held in both places of worship until 1956 when the Free Church was sold. It is now used as a community hall.

Park Village, Deeside.

A road linking the Deeside turnpike to the Parish of Durris via Park Bridge was laid out by the Deeside Railway Company in order to encourage passengers and freight from the south side of the river. A metal plate on the south-west girder of the bridge reads 'James Abernethy & Co., Ferryhill Foundry, Aberdeen, 1854'. Pontage of a ha'penny for a foot passenger, a penny for a passenger with a bicycle, and threepence for a car was charged for the use of the bridge, which was the last toll bridge in Aberdeenshire. The tollhouse on the north bank can clearly be seen in this picture. British Rail continued to collect the tolls right up to the mid-1950s. On a wooded mound at the south end of the bridge is an octagonal tower (erroneously called Keith's Tower) erected in 1825 by the Duke of Gordon to commemorate his acquisition of the estate of Durris after a protracted lawsuit. It was on the north bank of the river in an area still known as Keith's Muir that in the fourteenth century a fierce engagement took place between the Irvines of Drum and the Keiths, Great Marischals of Scotland who had estates on the south bank. Victory went to the Irvines, but the marriage of Alexander, son of Sir Alexander Irvine (who was killed at the Battle of Harlaw in 1411) to Elizabeth Keith, daughter of the then Great Marishal, made the victory academic and brought the feud to an end. In 2002 the spirit of friendship was marked by a ceremony which took place on the bridge between Michael Keith, Earl of Kintore and Chief of the Clan Keith, and David Irvine, 26th Laird of Drum.

The lands of Durris have a long association with Scottish kings. On his march north in 1296, Edward I of England stayed overnight at the nearby motte and bailey Castle of Durris (now only a mound) and was reported to have an army of 30,000 men at arms and 5,000 knights. Not surprisingly he received homage from the local lairds. The present Durris House is built around a tower dating from 1620. A famous previous owner was Dr James 'Paraffin' Young, the shale oil pioneer who bought the house and estate in 1871. He was a close friend and financial supporter of David Livingstone. In 1890 the Durris estate was bought by Mr H. R. Baird who continued the tradition of planting specimen trees as well as the management of young conifer forests. The portico shown in the picture was demolished in 1948 and the house has now been subdivided into several properties.

This private Episcopalian chapel was built at Durris in the mid-1890s to meet the wishes of Mrs Baird of Durris House. The nearest Episcopalian church was at Banchory – seven miles away or nearly an hour's drive. The charge was initially served by James Stuart, the curate of St Peter's Church in Torry, Aberdeen. From 1910 chaplains were appointed each summer and many well-known clergymen were invited to take services for a month with accommodation provided at nearby Nether Balfour House. In 1933 the chapel was closed and the building moved to serve a new community in Aberdeen.

KIRKTON EXCHANGE, DURRIS.

The hamlet of Kirkton of Durris was able to support a shop, which opened on 1 June 1886. In the early twentieth century there were only two telephones in the parish of Durris, one at the shop, which also doubled as the post office, and one at Durris House. The shop, which has now reverted to a private dwelling, was provided with a telephone kiosk in 1938.

Crathes station marks the end of this journey along Lower Deeside. Originally a halt to serve Crathes Castle, the station proper was built in 1863. A condition of the feu charter granted to the railway company for the building of the public station at Crathes was that all trains should stop there. This led to a dispute between Sir Robert Burnett of Crathes and the railway company. 'Messenger' trains ran on the line from 1865 to 1937 carrying despatches to Queen Victoria and later kings at Balmoral. By 1878 these services were being included in timetables (and carrying passengers) and in 1883 this led to a lawsuit because these trains, and also an excursion train to Banchory, were not stopping at Crathes. The railway company initially won the case but this victory was partially reversed in 1885 following an appeal to the House of Lords. It was ruled that the messenger trains had to make a stop at Crathes but the excursion services were allowed to pass through as they were not available to passengers with ordinary tickets. In 1914 Sir Thomas Burnett waived his rights and as a result some of the fast trains no longer stopped at Crathes. In 1969, after the line had closed, Malcolm Appleby, the renowned engraver and silversmith, bought the old station and made it his home and workshop for the next 27 years.